Freedom

Program Authors

Connie Juel, Ph.D.

Jeanne R. Paratore, Ed.D.

Deborah Simmons, Ph.D.

Sharon Vaughn, Ph.D.

ISBN: 0-328-21491-4
Copyright © 2008 Pearson Education, Inc.

5 6 7 8 9 10 V011 12 11 10 09 08 07
CC1

Editorial Offices: Glenview, Illinois • Parsippany, New Jersey • New York, New York
Sales Offices: Boston, Massachusetts • Duluth, Georgia • Glenview, Illinois
Coppell, Texas • Sacramento, California • Mesa, Arizona

Freedom

American Symbols

5

What are some important American symbols or monuments?

Animal Freedom **31**

What can we do to help animals?

American Symbols

American Symbols

Let's Explore

Words 2 the Wise

We have many **American symbols.** As you read this week's selections, think about what you know about these symbols. What do they tell us about America?

Let's Explore

Symbols of Freedom

What do you think of when people talk about the United States? Do you think of the stars on our flag? Or how about an eagle? The United States has many symbols. These symbols represent our history. They remind us of our rights. These symbols make people feel proud. Let's look at how some of these symbols came about.

The Bald Eagle

The bald eagle became a national symbol in 1782. Benjamin Franklin wanted our national bird to be the turkey. The government decided on the bald eagle. It is a symbol of strength, courage, and freedom.

Have you seen pictures of the bald eagle? It is on buildings. It is on our money. Many people around the world know the eagle is a symbol of the United States.

The Liberty Bell

The Liberty Bell rang on many special occasions. But the most famous time was on July 4, 1776. The bell was rung to call the citizens. There was a public reading announcing our desire to be a free country. The colonies wanted to be free from English rule. Have you seen pictures of the Liberty Bell? Many groups have used it as their symbol.

Uncle Sam

Uncle Sam has a white beard. He wears a red, white, and blue top hat. This symbol came about because of a man named Sam Wilson. Sam Wilson sent barrels of food to the troops. The barrels were marked "U.S." Someone said that U.S. stood for "Uncle Sam" Wilson. Soon artists were drawing pictures of Uncle Sam as a symbol of liberty.

She Stands for Freedom

by Diane L. Landsman

The Statue of Liberty stands in New York Harbor. The harbor is in New York City. Many people call the statue Lady Liberty. Lady Liberty wears a tall crown. She holds a torch in one hand. She holds a book in the other.

The statue was a gift from France in 1886. It was a sign of friendship. Nobody knew that it would become an important symbol. This famous monument stands for freedom for millions of people.

The Statue of Liberty is a symbol of freedom.

Why Is She Green?

The Statue of Liberty is made from copper. Copper is a strong material that won't rust. So why is the statue green? The statue stands near water. The weather and the water make the copper turn green. This is called *patina* (puh-TEE-nuh).

Lady Liberty's Journey

Artist Frédéric Auguste Bartholdi (FRED-er-ik aw-GUST bar-TOHL-dee) was a French sculptor. He made the Statue of Liberty in France. It was his idea to make a very large statue. He built it in pieces. It took ten years to make the pieces.

The sculptor had to plan how the enormous statue would get to America. He packed the pieces into 214 special cases. Then he put them on a ship.

Workers build the base for the Statue of Liberty.

The ship reached New York Harbor 27 days later. American workers put the statue together on Liberty Island. It was like an enormous puzzle. It took a year to put together.

What's Her Real Name?

Bartholdi named his statue *Liberty Enlightening the World*. He hoped that the statue would remind people of the importance of freedom. People began calling it the Statue of Liberty.

A celebration was held in New York Harbor for the Statue of Liberty.

Liberty Enlightening the World, Edward Moran, 1886.
© Museum of the City of New York.

Lady Liberty's Job

Bartholdi added many symbols to the statue. Her torch lights the way to freedom. Her foot is stepping on broken chains. The chains are symbols of freedom. The book in her left hand shows the date July 4, 1776. This is America's Independence Day. Lady Liberty's crown has seven points. Each point stands for the light of freedom shining on the seven seas and the seven continents.

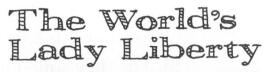

The World's Lady Liberty

Ellis Island is in New York Harbor. Ellis Island was the first stop for many immigrants coming to the United States.

Millions of immigrants passed through here from all over the world. They were looking for freedom. They were looking for opportunity. They wanted to live and work in America.

How Does She Stay Clean?

Cleaning tall statues and monuments is a dangerous job. Cleaners have to climb very high. Some hang from rope harnesses.

The Statue of Liberty was cleaned in the 1980s. Workers sprayed the statue with baking soda to remove layers of dirt.

Immigrants saw the statue's kind face as they sailed to Ellis Island. Lady Liberty held her torch high. It filled the immigrants with hope. It inspired them to dream of a better life. No one could have predicted what it would be like to see Lady Liberty. But most felt excited.

Lady Liberty was a special gift. It shows friendship and represents freedom. And it reminds people of our commitment to freedom.

commitment
dedication or promise

How Big Is Lady Liberty?

★ Height from the ground to top of her torch: 305 feet

★ Length of her index finger: 8 feet

★ Length of her nose: 4 feet 6 inches

★ Length of her right arm: 42 feet

★ Total weight of statue: 225 tons (450,000 pounds)

★ Weight of one fingernail: 3.5 pounds

★ Windows in her crown: 25

★ Steps to climb from toe to crown: 354

What Do You Think?

Why is the Statue of Liberty a famous symbol of the United States?

The Men on the

Imagine that you were asked to create a great symbol for our nation. The United States wanted you to carve giant statues into the tall Black Hills of South Dakota. Sound difficult? Now imagine how long it would take.

One sculptor took this job in 1923. He was Gutzon Borglum (GOOT-zon BOR-gluhm).

Gutzon Borglum was chosen to design Mount Rushmore.

Mountain

by Joseph R. Frederick

The government told him that people from all over the world would travel to South Dakota to see Mount Rushmore.

Borglum decided the statues should show America's Presidents. He chose George Washington, Thomas Jefferson, Theodore Roosevelt, and Abraham Lincoln. The monument would be a symbol of liberty. Let's learn more about these men.

George Washington
(1732 - 1799)

George Washington was the first President of the United States. He was known for his patience and understanding. He believed in liberty for all.

Many people in the United States loved Washington. Henry Lee fought in the Revolutionary War with Washington. Lee said this about him: "First in war, first in peace, and first in the hearts of his countrymen." People call Washington the "Father of Our Country."

Thomas Jefferson
(1743 – 1826)

Thomas Jefferson was the third President of the United States. He wrote the Declaration of Independence. We celebrate the signing of this document every Fourth of July.

Jefferson was very talented. He was a lawyer, a musician, and a successful architect. He designed large buildings in his home state of Virginia. Some of these include the University of Virginia and the Virginia state capitol.

Abraham Lincoln
(1809 - 1865)

Abraham Lincoln was the sixteenth President of the United States. Lincoln was the tallest President. He was six feet four inches tall. He was President during the Civil War. The war was fought over slavery. Lincoln ended slavery so all Americans would be free and equal. Lincoln also believed that the country should stay together. He believed in the United States and in democracy.

Theodore Roosevelt
(1858 - 1919)

Theodore Roosevelt was the twenty-sixth President of the United States. He was also the youngest President.

Theodore Roosevelt loved the outdoors. He enjoyed riding horses, swimming, hunting, and hiking. He worked hard to create national parks and protect forests.

Americans called him "Teddy" as a nickname. Once he was photographed with a bear. The teddy bear was named after him.

Roosevelt was the first President to ride in a car, an airplane, and a submarine.

Facing History

Mount Rushmore was the perfect place for the statues. Borglum and a crew of stone carvers began working on the mountain in 1927.

The men blasted away huge pieces of granite with dynamite. Then they shaped the features by hand. They used instruments such as drills, air hammers, and chisels. It was dirty and dangerous work.

Granite a very hard rock used for buildings and monuments

Mount Rushmore took fourteen years to finish. The four heads are each sixty feet high. George Washington was done first. Jefferson and Lincoln followed. Roosevelt's head was finished last. Their faces can be seen from sixty miles away.

Mount Rushmore National Memorial is very popular. More than twenty thousand people a day view the memorial in the summer.

Mount Rushmore Time Line

1927 Carving begins on Mount Rushmore.

1930 Head of George Washington unveiled.

1936 Head of Thomas Jefferson unveiled.

1937 Head of Abraham Lincoln unveiled.

1939 Head of Theodore Roosevelt unveiled.

1941 Sculptor Gutzon Borglum dies; his son finishes the sculpture.

What Do You Think?

Why is Mount Rushmore an important national monument?

Stars and Stripes

Each part of the American flag has a meaning. The stripes stand for the thirteen original colonies. There are seven red stripes and six white stripes. The fifty stars are symbols for the fifty states. The stars are on a blue background.

But this country's flag didn't always look this way. There were different flags over time.

The American Flag Through History

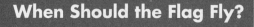

The Betsy Ross Flag (1776)
This was the first "stars and stripes" flag. It was sewn in Philadelphia.

The Bennington Flag (1777)
This flag was flown at the Battle of Bennington in Vermont.

The 1818 Flag
The government decided to add one star for each state. A star was added for each new state.

The American Flag Today
Alaska and Hawaii won statehood in 1959. Now there are fifty stars.

When Should the Flag Fly?

New Year's Day January 1

Inauguration Day January 20

Martin Luther King Jr.'s Birthday
Third Monday in January

Lincoln's Birthday February 12

Washington's Birthday
Third Monday in February

Patriot's Day September 11

Memorial Day

Flag Day June 14

Independence Day July 4

Labor Day

Constitution Day September 17

Columbus Day Second Monday in October

Veterans Day November 11

Thanksgiving Day

4 You 2 Do

Word Play

Unscramble the letters to spell the names of six American symbols of freedom.

AUTEST FO RITELYB   LDBA GEAEL

LUCEN MAS   UNTOM MURHOSER

EMAIRNAC GLFA   BELTIRY LELB

Making Connections

Imagine that monuments could communicate with each other! Choose to be Lady Liberty or one of the Presidents on Mount Rushmore. Explain to the other statues about why you are a great symbol of freedom.

On Paper

The American flag is a symbol of our country. The stars and stripes have meanings too. Design a flag for your school. Explain the meanings of the symbols you use in your flag.

Answers for Word Play: column 1: Statue of Liberty, Uncle Sam, American Flag; column 2: bald eagle, Mount Rushmore, Liberty Bell

30

Animal Freedom

Contents

Animal Freedom

Let's Explore

Words 2 the Wise

Animals need our help to protect their health and their freedom. Think about **animal freedom** and what that means as you read this week's selections.

Gene and Lorri Bauston rescued a sick sheep in 1986. They named her Hilda. This gave them the idea for the Farm Sanctuary (SANK-choo-air-ee). A sanctuary is a place where animals can be safe from harm. The Farm Sanctuary helps farm animals that have been hurt or badly treated. Now there are two Farm Sanctuary locations. One is in New York. The other is in California.

This baby calf lost her mother.

Sanctuary

The animals live in clean areas. They eat a healthy diet. They run and play in the fields. They get lots of love and attention from staff and visitors. They even have an animal doctor.

The Farm Sanctuary has over 100,000 members. Millions of people learn about these farm animals through television and newspapers. They share information about projects and animal treatment. Visitors can tour and stay overnight at the Sanctuary.

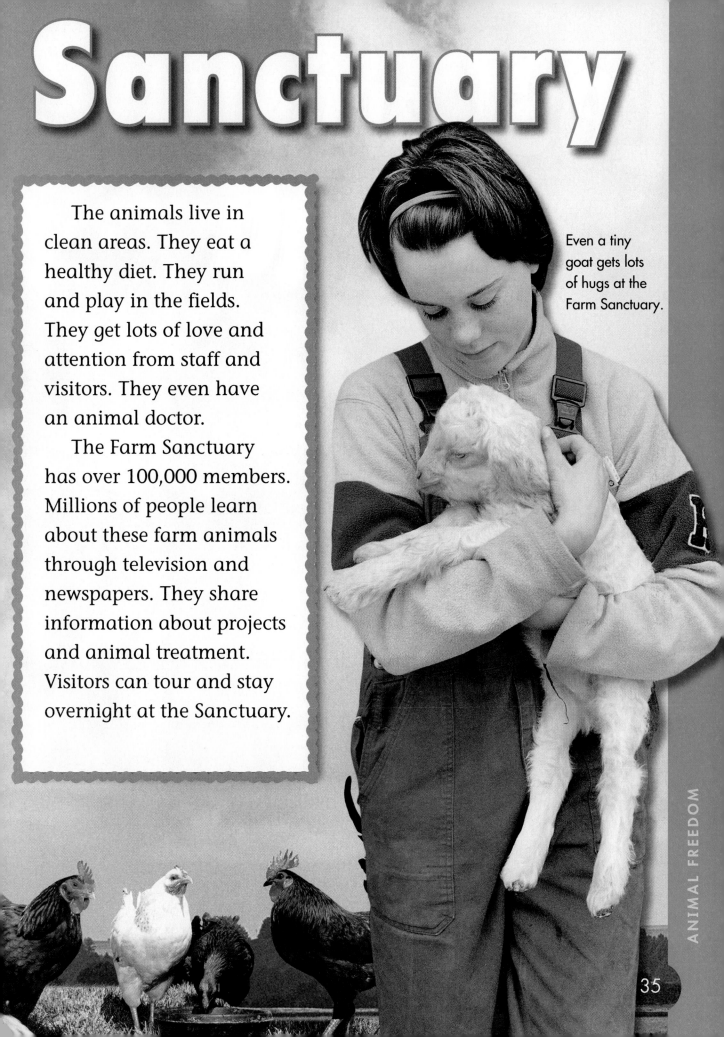

Even a tiny goat gets lots of hugs at the Farm Sanctuary.

Lost and Found

Wake-Up!

A day at an animal shelter is busy. It starts with feeding all of the animals. Some animals need medicine. The staff gives them medicine with their breakfast. The staff is made up of the people who work at the shelter. They make sure each animal stays healthy.

Check-In!

Each day the staff checks in new animals. Sometimes people bring dogs, cats, or other animals to the shelter. They come to the shelter to give the animals a safe home.

The staff writes a short report for each animal. This report describes the type of animal. It also tells where the animal was found.

Animals that are brought to the shelter are placed on a list of missing pets. It is helpful for people who want to adopt a pet too.

Time for Exercise!

The animals need exercise. The staff uses an outdoor space near the shelter. Some shelters do not have a lot of space. Animals there are taken for walks. More space means more comfort.

Health Matters!

The animals are out for exercise. This is a good time for their cages to be cleaned. Shelters do all they can to keep each animal healthy. Clean cages help animals stay healthy. Fresh water is important too.

Animal doctors are called veterinarians, or vets. They provide care to sick animals.

Veterinarians may work for a shelter. Or they may volunteer their time. Vets check the animals' health. They give the animals a check-up just like the doctors do for people. Some animals may need surgery. Some may need to be on a different diet.

The vets hope all animals at the shelter will find the comfort of a new home.

What's the Count?

The number of animals that each shelter keeps is different. It depends on the space and money. That's why shelters need volunteers. Volunteers help feed and care for animals. They help by petting the animals. Or they help by taking a pet for a walk. A volunteer has to really love animals.

Shelters also need donations. A donation is money that people give. It helps to pay for the food and care of the animals.

Do you know how many animals are taken in by shelters each year? It is between 6 and 8 million animals! That is a lot of animals that need homes. Is it a good idea to visit a shelter if you want a pet? Yes! If you are looking for a special animal friend, visit an animal shelter. The right pet is waiting for you!

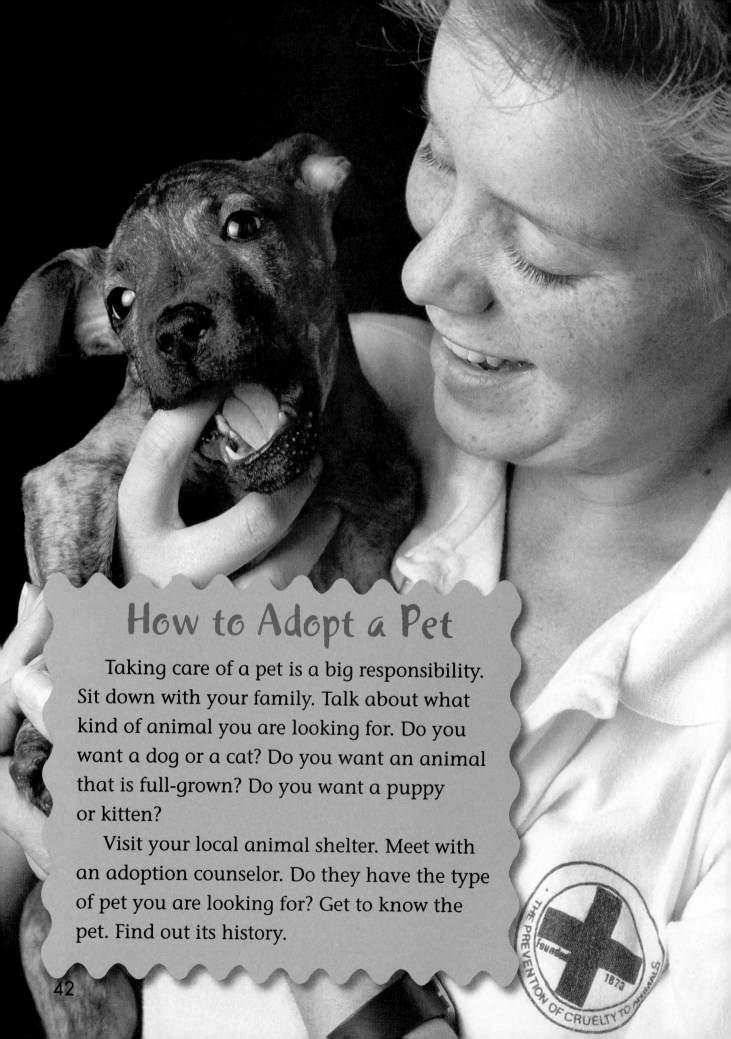

How to Adopt a Pet

Taking care of a pet is a big responsibility. Sit down with your family. Talk about what kind of animal you are looking for. Do you want a dog or a cat? Do you want an animal that is full-grown? Do you want a puppy or kitten?

Visit your local animal shelter. Meet with an adoption counselor. Do they have the type of pet you are looking for? Get to know the pet. Find out its history.

Groups that Care

There are many groups that work to give animals happy homes. Contact groups like the Humane Society or Petfinder. They share information and watch out for animals.

The Internet is another way to find groups that help pets. Petfinder and World Animal Net both have good Web sites.

Be a friend to animals. Contact an animal shelter if you see a hurt animal in your neighborhood.

What Do You Think?

What are the steps you take to adopt a pet?

43

CRITTERS IN THE CORN PATCH

By William Lindsay • Illustrated by Daniel Powers

I love corn on the cob. I love it with salt and dripping with butter. It just so happens that my Grandpa Joe grows the best sweet corn in the state of New York. People drive for miles just to buy it.

People are not the only ones who enjoy the taste of corn. Raccoons love corn too. Grandpa Joe says that the world's biggest, hungriest, corn-loving raccoons live on his farm.

"Those raccoons are at it again," he shouted. This was last summer when I was visiting the farm. He wiped his muddy boots on the doormat. He shook an ear of corn that the raccoons had nibbled on during the night.

"They broke twenty stalks!" Grandpa complained. "They tried to climb to the top to get the very best ears. It's time to outsmart these corn-eating critters once and for all."

He had an idea.

He disappeared into his workshop. He spent the rest of the day there. I heard him sawing wood and hammering nails.

Grandpa Joe came into the kitchen before dinner to show off his work. He carried what looked like a tiny wooden jail. It was a raccoon trap! Grandma looked worried.

"I won't hurt them," he said quickly. "I won't be cruel. I just want to capture them."

"Here's how it works. The raccoon eats the bait. It triggers a spring. The door snaps shut. The raccoon won't be able to get out no matter how hard it struggles. I'll take the ones I capture far away before I let them go. That will teach them to stop eating my corn."

Grandpa Joe spread some peanut butter on an apple. Then he put it in the trap as bait.

"That ought to taste good to a hungry raccoon," Grandpa chuckled. He and I went out to set his trap. He walked into the corn patch with his trap. I waited on the patio.

The door on the trap was shut tight the next day. But there was no raccoon inside!

It had chewed through the wooden bars and escaped. You know where it went? Right into Grandpa's corn patch! Stalks were bent and twisted everywhere.

Grandpa Joe marched into his workshop. He didn't come out until lunchtime.

He walked into the kitchen with a big grin. His trap didn't look the same. It was covered with steel.

"Let's see that old raccoon chew through this," said Grandpa.

We hurried out to the garden with the new trap. This time we baited it with hot dogs (my idea). We also put in a piece of Grandma's apple pie. This would provide a special treat.

The next morning Grandpa Joe and I raced out to the corn patch. The trap was all locked up. We could hear scratching and clawing. The animal was putting up a struggle. Grandpa Joe was happy.

We loaded the trap into the back of Grandpa's truck. We drove to a big forest. We hiked into the woods with the trap.

We walked for a very long time. We stopped in a small clearing near some trees.

"This is the perfect spot," said Grandpa Joe. "The berries and nuts will provide this raccoon with lots to eat."

Grandpa Joe unlocked the trap. Then he shook it to set the animal free.

"Come on out!" he yelled. He put his face down close to the door. Suddenly, Grandpa Joe jumped up with a shout. He started running. I ran too.

I looked back. And the biggest skunk I ever saw walked out of that steel-covered trap!

WHAT DO YOU THINK?

What steps did Grandpa Joe take to trap the animal?

RUNNING FREE

Did you know that horses are naturally wild? They love to run free. Horses are intelligent creatures. Horses have developed over millions of years.

Did you also know that wild horses are herd animals? In a herd, animals eat together and move to new places together. A herd is like a family. Horse herds are called bands.

There used to be thousands of wild horses in the United States. There are still wild horses today, but not as many. Farmers want to use land for raising cattle. So wild horses are being rounded up.

Wild horses live in eleven different western states. Montana and North Dakota are two of the states where wild horses live. The United States government owns and cares for most of this land.

Sable Island, Shackleford Island, and Cumberland Island are islands where wild horses can be found.

Some people have created wild horse sanctuaries. These places provide horses with a safe place to live. They are fed and cared for and allowed to run free with their herd families. Groups like the Fund for Animals and Wild Horses Freedom Alliance work to change laws. They want horse roundups to end. They want wild horses to be able to run free again.

Word Play

A synonym is a word that has the same or almost the same meaning as another word. What are some synonyms for these words?

provide   comfort   capture

Making Connections

The Farm Sanctuary and animal shelters try to find safe homes for animals. What types of animals need safe homes in the city? What types of animals need safe homes outside of the city?

On Paper

What could you do to help the wild animals that live in your neighborhood?

Possible answers for Word Play: provide—give, supply; comfort—cheer, calm; capture—catch, trap

EXPRESSING YOURSELF

Contents

EXPRESSING YOURSELF

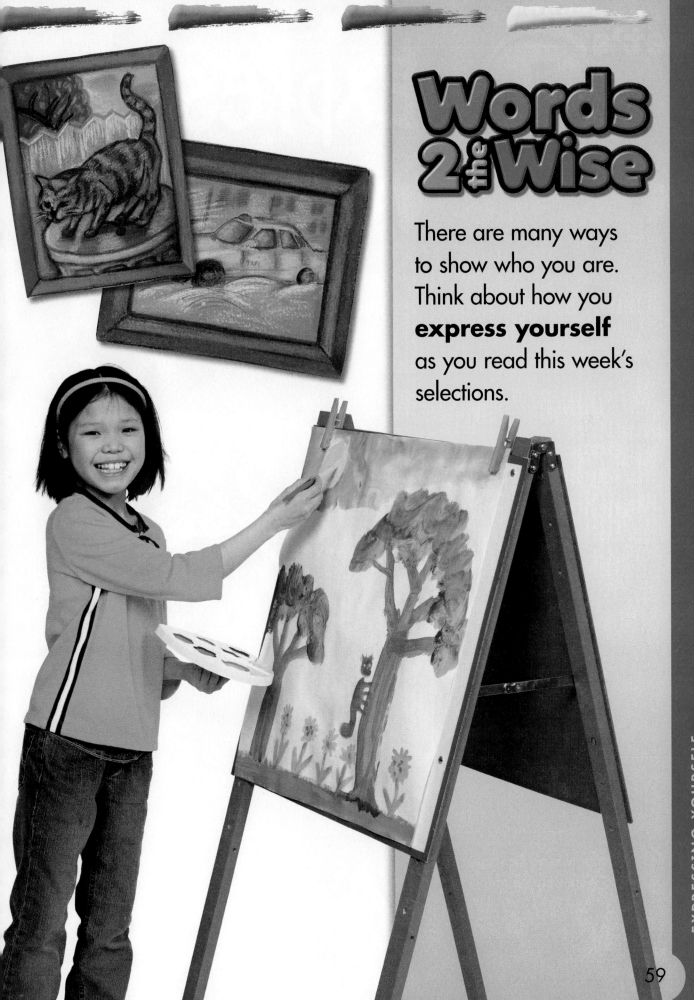

Words 2 the Wise

There are many ways to show who you are. Think about how you **express yourself** as you read this week's selections.

Expressing Yourself

How do you show who you are? Is it by how you dress? Is it by what you create? Is it by what you like to do? Self-expression is letting others see who you really are.

Some people express who they are by how they dress or wear their hair. Some people like to draw, paint, or build things. Some people like to dance, sing, or act.

Performing on the stage is one way to share who you are.

What do you like to do? Who or what inspires you? Let your imagination go wild. Picture yourself singing in front of your classmates. Or imagine yourself writing a story that makes people laugh. Whatever you choose, dare to dream and express the real you!

Words work out your ideas and express your true thoughts.

Sometimes the tools used to create are found outdoors.

61

Not a Typical THEATER

What do eight-foot-tall puppets, talking lizards, and dancing monkeys have in common? You can see them all at Redmoon Theater in Chicago. Have you ever seen a lady sitting on a six-foot high stool while riding on top of a tractor? You would if you saw a Redmoon Theater play called *Nina*.

Redmoon Theater puts on plays that inspire people to try new things.

People that perform at Redmoon Theater have very unusual talents!

Redmoon Theater began in 1989. Since then it has put on over 60 shows in more than 30 places. Many theaters put on shows on stages only. But Redmoon Theater puts on shows in parks, on streets, and even on the steps of a museum.

Puppets are used in many of the plays. Some puppets are so big that a person can fit inside.

This production took place outdoors. What do you think it was about?

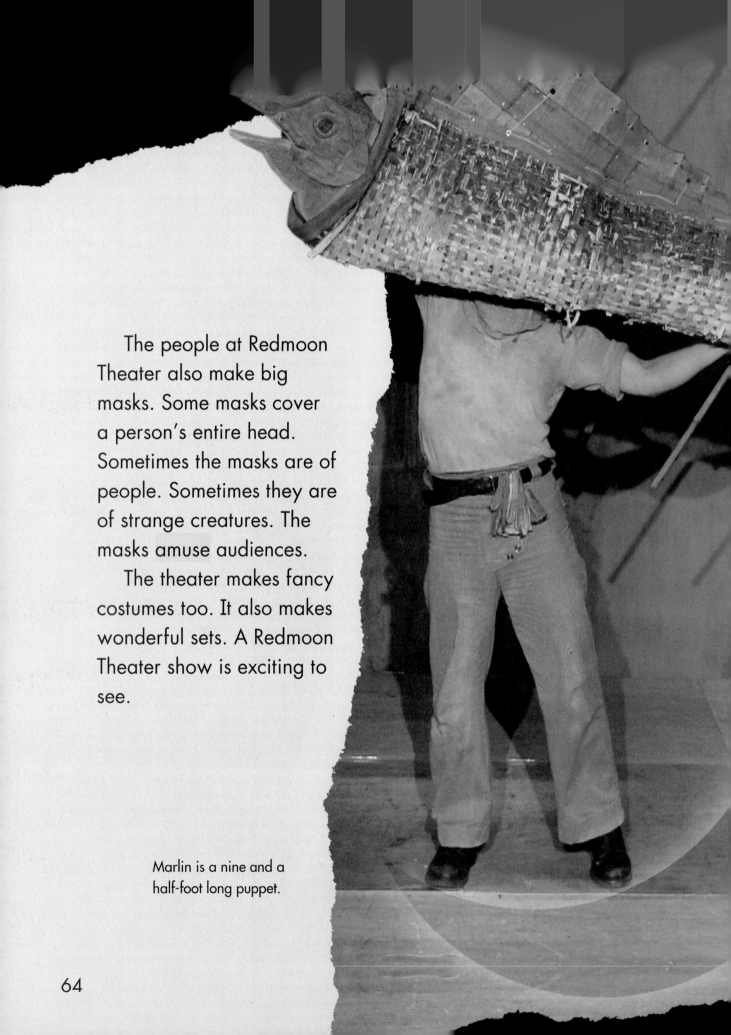

The people at Redmoon Theater also make big masks. Some masks cover a person's entire head. Sometimes the masks are of people. Sometimes they are of strange creatures. The masks amuse audiences.

The theater makes fancy costumes too. It also makes wonderful sets. A Redmoon Theater show is exciting to see.

Marlin is a nine and a half-foot long puppet.

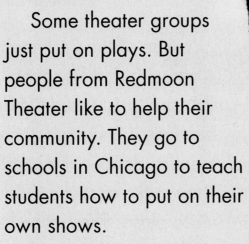

Some theater groups just put on plays. But people from Redmoon Theater like to help their community. They go to schools in Chicago to teach students how to put on their own shows.

The students learn about stage makeup and costumes. They learn about making sets. They learn about acting. They pick the show they want to put on. In the spring, the students put on their very own play.

Actors from Redmoon Theater teach kids what it takes to be a performer.

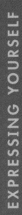

Some of the Redmoon people work with middle school students. This group is called "Dramagirls" because it is for girls only. They learn to dance. They learn to act. They make costumes. And they write plays. They even learn to walk on stilts! These girls might have a future in the theater.

Dramagirls: DRAH-muh-gerlz

Redmoon believes that performing powerful actions, such as stilt-walking, drumming, and acting, creates powerful performers.

Some of Redmoon's presentations are a yearly tradition. For eight years they held a lantern parade. One year, hundreds of people came to see a performance of the parade.

They also have a winter show. There are puppets and other wonderful things in the show. But these are not like puppets you might have at home. One year they even had a stampede of buffalo puppets.

A snow queen serves tea in the winter show.

In the shows, they use props no one is expecting. Props are things such as chairs, dishes, and food that make a play seem more real. Sometimes they walk on stilts and carry banners. Sometimes they act inside giant puppets. Sometimes they dance in the streets.

These performers created horses out of buckets, brooms, bottle caps, and rope.

Redmoon Theater people express themselves in all sorts of ways. But they don't just amuse people. They like to inspire people and make them think too.

The people of Redmoon Theater believe in being free to express the magic that is inside of all of us.

What Do You THINK?

What kind of a play would you like to perform in a park? How would your play change if you performed it on a stage?

What makes an Artist?

by Michael Archer • illustrated by Susan Tolonen

Kim Chang stood near the display of photos. She was proud of her blue ribbon.

"I don't get it. Why did *those* win first place?" a voice behind her said. "They're just a bunch of photos of trash."

Kim turned around. "Frank! I thought you said you didn't care who won the contest?"

"I don't. I just thought the judges would love my drawings," Frank said sadly.

"I worked really hard on the drawings. You just took a picture with the click of a button. You didn't create anything," he added.

Kim had three winning photos. One showed a picture of an alley cat waiting to pounce. Another photo was of a garbage can tipped over with colorful containers spilling out. The third was of a yellow taxicab splashing through puddles on a rainy day.

Kim looked at her photos. She had spent hours carefully picking out the best shots from her many rolls of film.

"It's more than just pushing a button," she told Frank. "Photography is art too."

"I think of art as drawings or paintings," Frank said firmly. "Not photos."

Kim looked at all the other entries. They were all paintings and drawings. Was Frank right?

"I guess the judges didn't think so," she said.

Kim was upset. She wanted to go home. As she turned around, she stepped on a woman's foot. The woman had been standing there the whole time.

"I'm sorry," said Kim.

"That's all right," the woman said. "Did I hear you say these photos are yours?"

"Yes," Kim said.

"They're very good. You have a lot of talent," she said. "You are a real artist."

"Who are you?" Frank asked.

"My name is Roberta Childs," the woman replied.

"*The* Roberta Childs?" Kim asked. "Wow! I love the photos you took in Africa."

"Thank you," said Ms. Childs.

"What are you doing here?" asked Kim.

"I'm visiting a friend. Her little girl has a drawing on display."

"Don't you think that a *drawing* shows whether someone is a good artist or not?" Frank asked.

"No. Artists can paint, draw, take photos, build things, write, sing and lots of other things." said Ms. Childs.

"Artists see things in a different way," she said. "The tough part is how to express it."

Frank looked at his drawings of horses. In his mind he saw horses with wind whipping through their long manes. He wondered if he had shown that clearly.

"I think I understand what you mean," Frank said.

"But remember there are lots of ways to express what you see," Ms. Childs added.

"Have you seen any amazing buildings?" she asked.

"Yes, lots. Downtown and in other big cities," said Kim.

"Why?" asked Frank.

"Buildings are art too. Just like photographs, drawings, and paintings. Even furniture can be art! You are both artists, even if you have different ways to express yourselves."

"I'm glad your photos won, Kim," Frank said. "I'm going to find a new way to express the wild horses in my imagination."

Kim smiled. "We can be different, but both of us create art."

"I think so too," said Frank.

"Let's go enjoy another artistic creation," he said.

"What?" asked Kim.

"Giant ice cream sundaes."

"OK, but don't tell me what to put on top of my sundae," Kim laughed.

What Do You Think?

How can two different things such as ice cream sundaes and photographs both show creativity?

Puppet Magic

Do you want to put on a puppet show? It's easy! Puppets can be made out of all kinds of things. Follow these quick and easy steps to make a paper-plate puppet. Then put on a show!

To make a paper-plate puppet
you will need the following items:

1. two paper plates

2. buttons

3. markers or crayons

4. yarn

5. construction paper

6. scissors

7. stapler

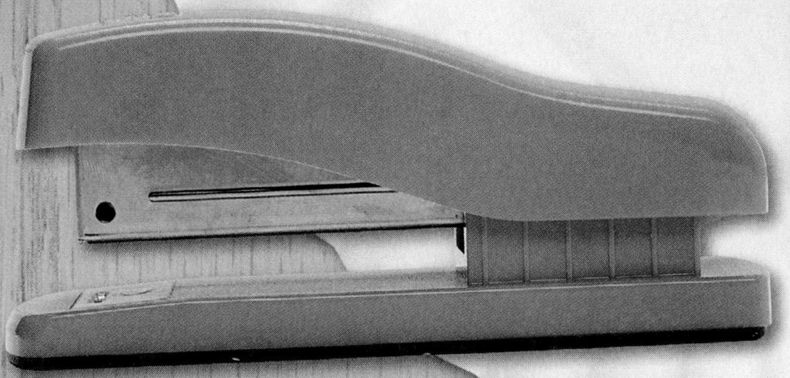

1 Staple two paper plates together. Make sure that the eating surfaces of the plates are facing each other. Also, leave a small space between the plates for your hand to fit into.

2 Where the two plates aren't stapled, cut across in a straight line. This is where you will put your hand to move the puppet.

3 Decorate your puppet. Use buttons for eyes and yarn for hair. You can use the construction paper to make legs, arms, or clothes for your puppet. Use your markers or crayons to color and bring your puppet to life.

One great place to put on a puppet show is in your living room. You can hide behind your couch. Raise your hand with the puppet above the couch so your audience sees only the puppet. Or you can cover a table with a tablecloth and sit behind the table. Rehearse your lines. Invite an audience. It's show time!

81

Word Play

You're putting on a puppet show! Write an ad for your show. Use as many of the words below as you can.

amuse   express
create   inspire
display   theater

Making Connections

How do theater groups, like the Redmoon Theater, and art contests like the one Kim and Frank entered, give people a chance to express themselves?

On Paper

Everyone has some way of expressing themselves. How do you like to express yourself?

It's the Law!

Contents

It's the Law!

Words 2 the Wise

It's the law that everyone in the United States has to obey our laws. As you read this week's selections, think about what you know about the law.

Let's Explore
The Bill of Rights

Many American leaders felt uneasy in 1789. Basic rights and freedoms were not included in the U.S. Constitution when it was written. There were some disagreements. So Congress wrote amendments. An amendment is an addition or change to the Constitution. The first ten amendments were passed in December 1791. Together, they are called the Bill of Rights.

The Bill of Rights includes these freedoms and rights.

- Freedom to practice your own religion

- Freedom of speech

- Freedom of the press

- Freedom to assemble

- Freedom to keep and bear arms

- Right of an accused person to a trial by jury

- The right against unreasonable searches and seizures

The Bill of Rights protects our most important freedoms. We've enjoyed these freedoms for over 200 years.

SOUND OFF

by Ellen Javernick

A Pollution Problem

When you "sound off" about something, you tell people what you think. Many people sound off about loud sounds.

Sounds that disturb us are called *noise*. The world is getting noisier all the time. More cars and trucks are on the road. This noise can annoy people.

Some people say noise is a health problem. Noise can cause hearing loss. It can make people feel worried. Many people want to make laws to stop noise pollution.

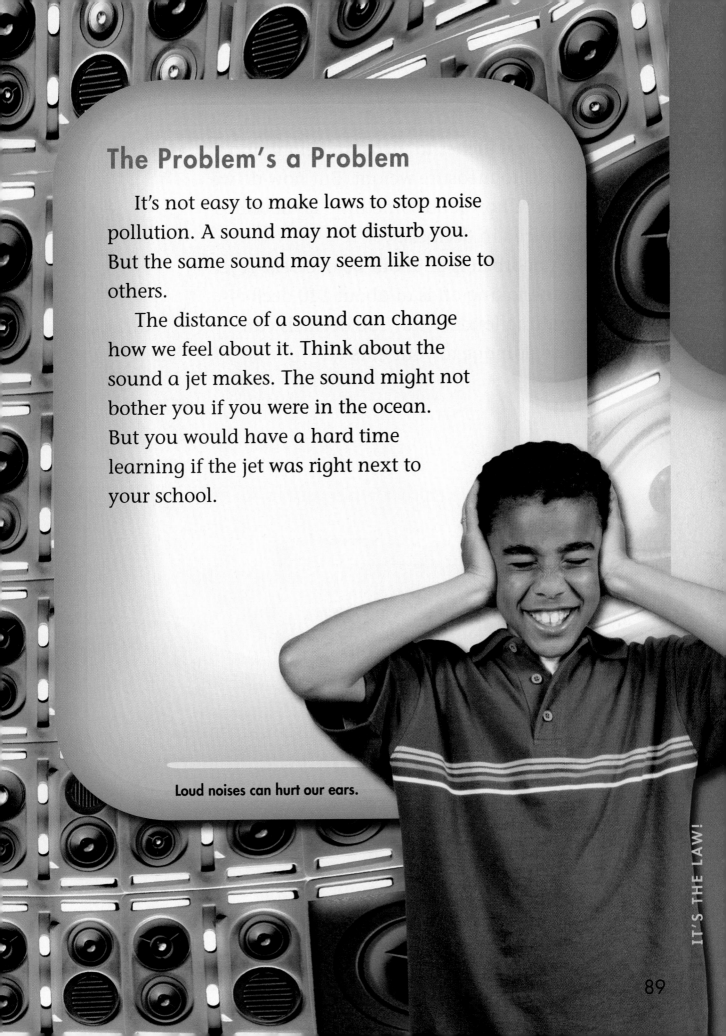

The Problem's a Problem

It's not easy to make laws to stop noise pollution. A sound may not disturb you. But the same sound may seem like noise to others.

The distance of a sound can change how we feel about it. Think about the sound a jet makes. The sound might not bother you if you were in the ocean. But you would have a hard time learning if the jet was right next to your school.

Loud noises can hurt our ears.

How Loud Is Loud?

We use inches to measure height and pounds to measure weight. But how do we measure how loud something is? Sound is measured in decibels.

A doorbell is at about 80 decibels. A jet engine taking off is at about 140 decibels. Anything louder than 150 decibels can cause damage to your ears.

decibels (DES-i-bels) dBA

Unbearable so painful that you cannot stand it

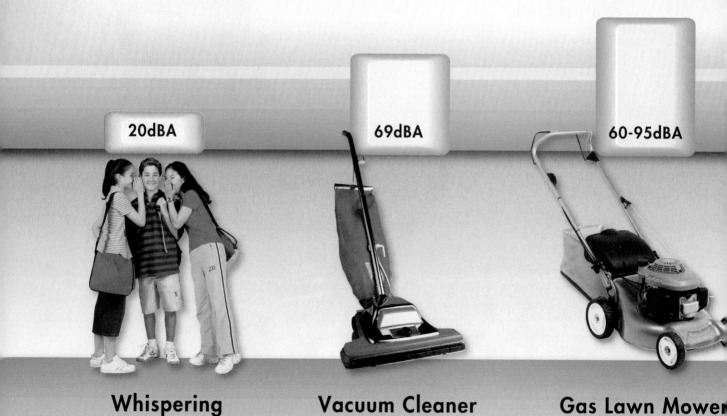

20dBA

69dBA

60-95dBA

Whispering　　　　**Vacuum Cleaner**　　　　**Gas Lawn Mower**

The chart on this page shows the noise levels of some common sounds. Sound of over 140 dBA can hurt our ears. It can hurt our ears even if we only hear it once.

Sound above 85 dBA hurts our ears if we hear it more than once. Even lower noise levels can bother us. Any noise can be unbearable at times.

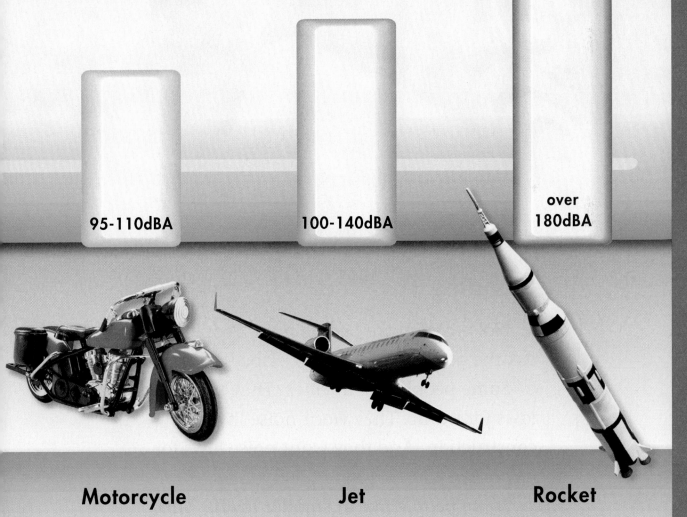

95-110dBA

100-140dBA

over 180dBA

Motorcycle

Jet

Rocket

Stopping The Noise

Noise can make people mad. People often ask the government to make noise laws.

Some people live in cities. They want noise laws for traffic. They want noise laws for construction. And they want noise laws for airports.

Some people live in smaller towns. They want noise laws for barking dogs. They also want noise laws for loud lawn mowers. Noise laws need to be fair to everyone.

Should There Be A Law?

Sometimes a new law will make everyone happy. Sometimes a new law will make everyone upset.

Imagine you were asked to make noise laws. Read the noise pollution problems on the next pages. What would you do? Remember to respect the rights of everyone involved.

1. There is an airport in town. People built new houses near the airport. The people who live in the houses want a new law. They want a law that will lower the noise pollution from airplanes. What will you do?

2. People have a dog that barks. The people who live next door want a law that will force the owners to pay money if the dog barks. What will you do?

3. Motorcycles have mufflers. The mufflers make the motorcycles quieter. Some riders take them off. Some people hate the noise. Those people want a law that riders must pay money if they take their mufflers off. What will you do?

4. Fire trucks, ambulances, and police cars have sirens on them. The sirens annoy some people at night. The sirens wake them up. Those people want a law that does not allow sirens at night. What will you do?

What Do You Think?

What is the main problem with noise pollution?

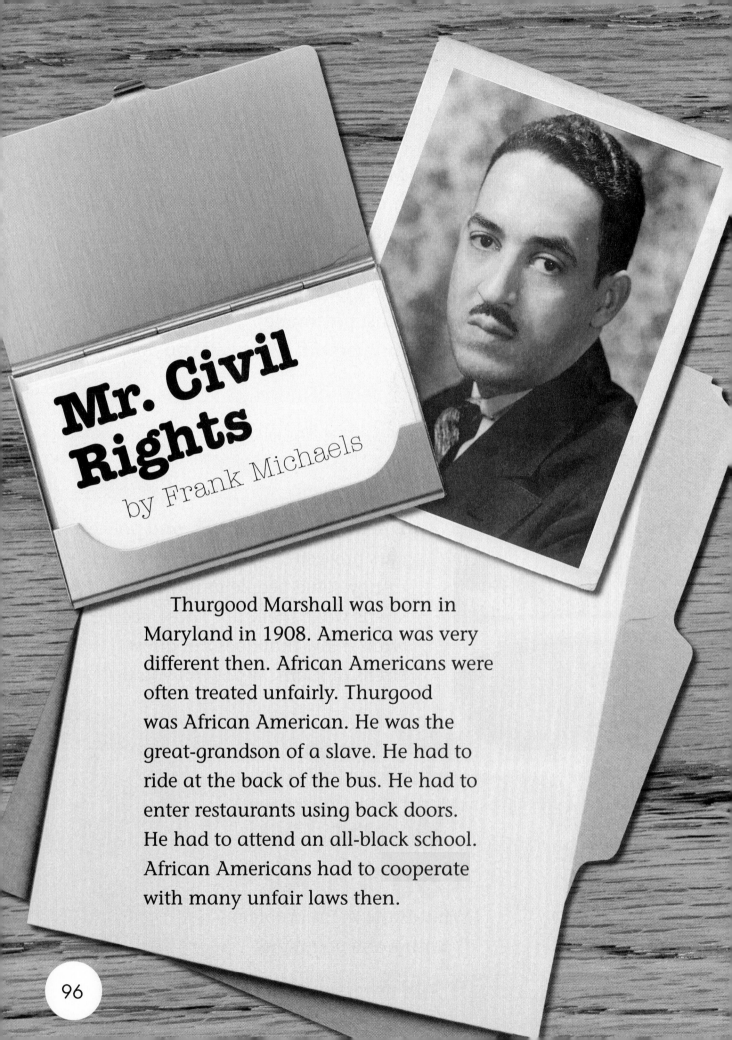

Mr. Civil Rights

by Frank Michaels

Thurgood Marshall was born in Maryland in 1908. America was very different then. African Americans were often treated unfairly. Thurgood was African American. He was the great-grandson of a slave. He had to ride at the back of the bus. He had to enter restaurants using back doors. He had to attend an all-black school. African Americans had to cooperate with many unfair laws then.

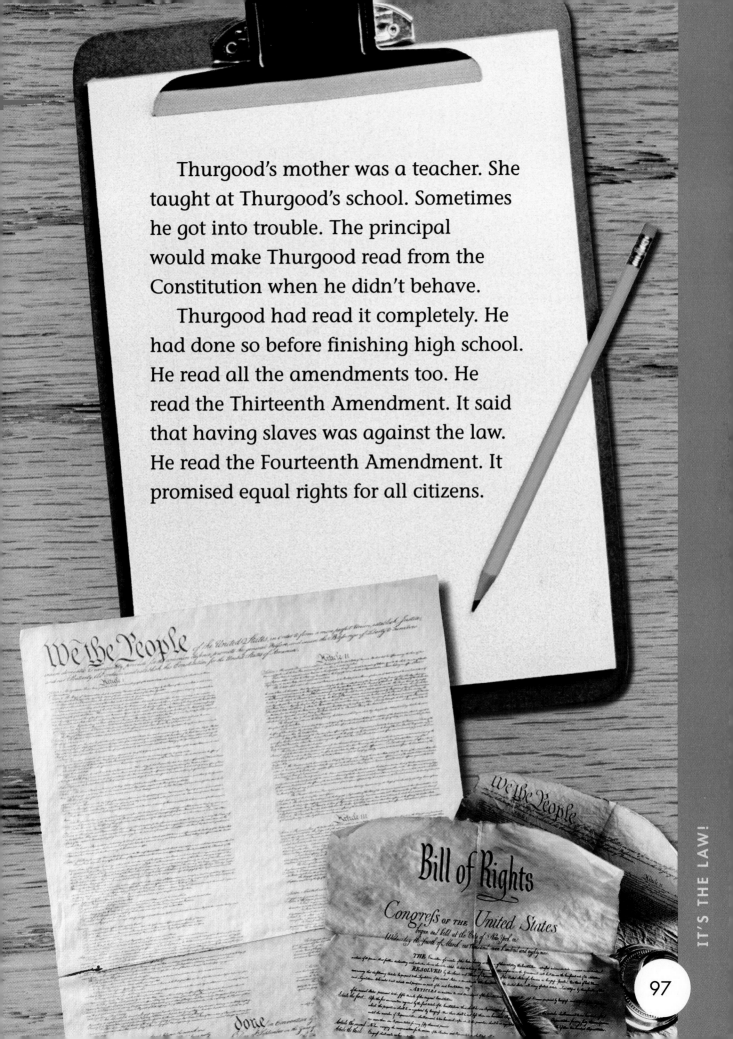

Thurgood's mother was a teacher. She taught at Thurgood's school. Sometimes he got into trouble. The principal would make Thurgood read from the Constitution when he didn't behave.

Thurgood had read it completely. He had done so before finishing high school. He read all the amendments too. He read the Thirteenth Amendment. It said that having slaves was against the law. He read the Fourteenth Amendment. It promised equal rights for all citizens.

Thurgood asked many questions. He wanted to know why black people didn't have the rights promised in the U.S. Constitution. His father told him that "what was in the Constitution was what ought to be, not what was." The people who wrote the Constitution had good intentions. But promises were not carried through for all people.

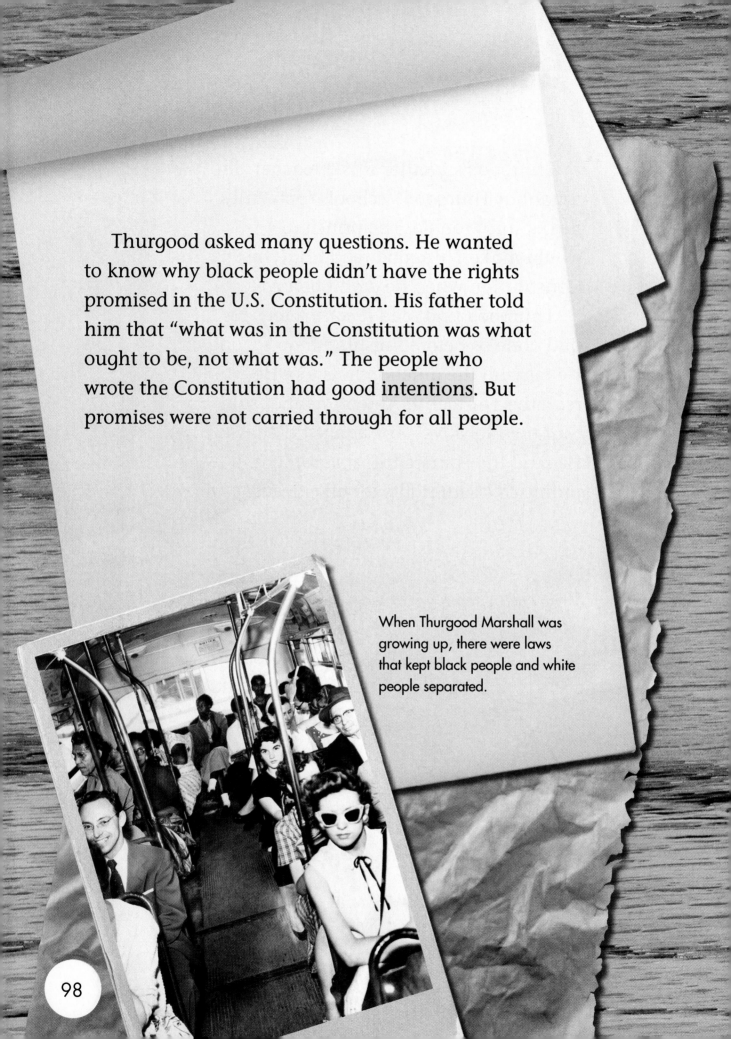

When Thurgood Marshall was growing up, there were laws that kept black people and white people separated.

Thurgood Marshall reads
to his son from a law book.

Thurgood's father was a waiter. He worked
at a white men's club. When he could, he spent
time with Thurgood. He would take him and
his older brother to the courthouse. They would
watch and listen to trials. Mr. Marshall never
told him to be a lawyer. But Thurgood said, "He
turned me into one. He did it by teaching me to
argue, by making me prove everything I said."

Thurgood wanted to fight unfairness.
He knew that he could in a courtroom.
So he decided to become a lawyer.

Thurgood was not allowed to attend the law school he first chose. It was because he was African American. He went to Howard University instead. It was an all-black school. His mother sold her wedding ring to help pay for his schooling.

The work at school was hard. But Thurgood said, "I heard law books were to dig in, so I dug, way deep." Thurgood finished law school in 1933. He was at the top of his class.

Thurgood Marshall (standing) works on a case.

Thurgood Marshall worked as legal director for the NAACP.

Thurgood soon opened a law office. He helped poor black people. One day one of his teachers from law school asked Thurgood for help. He asked if he'd be a lawyer for the National Association for the Advancement of Colored People (NAACP). The NAACP helped black people. The NAACP worked to make sure that black people had the same rights as white people. Thurgood cooperated. It was just what he wanted to do.

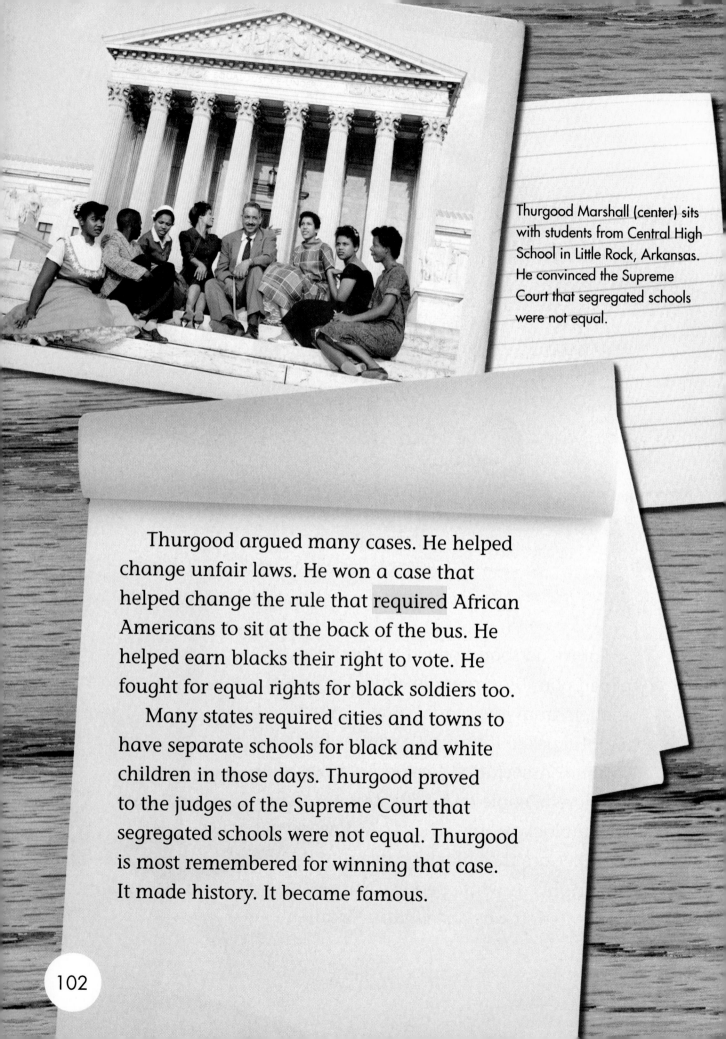

Thurgood Marshall (center) sits with students from Central High School in Little Rock, Arkansas. He convinced the Supreme Court that segregated schools were not equal.

Thurgood argued many cases. He helped change unfair laws. He won a case that helped change the rule that required African Americans to sit at the back of the bus. He helped earn blacks their right to vote. He fought for equal rights for black soldiers too.

Many states required cities and towns to have separate schools for black and white children in those days. Thurgood proved to the judges of the Supreme Court that segregated schools were not equal. Thurgood is most remembered for winning that case. It made history. It became famous.

Thurgood worked hard to make sure all people had the rights the Constitution promised. He won twenty-nine out of the thirty-two cases he brought before the Supreme Court. People called him Mr. Civil Rights.

In 1965 President Lyndon Johnson picked Thurgood to be the first black judge on the U.S. Supreme Court. The words on the front of the courthouse say "Equal Justice For All." Thurgood's intentions were that all people would have equal justice.

When he died in 1993, he was buried in Arlington National Cemetery. In 2003 the U.S. Postal Service printed a stamp in honor of this American hero.

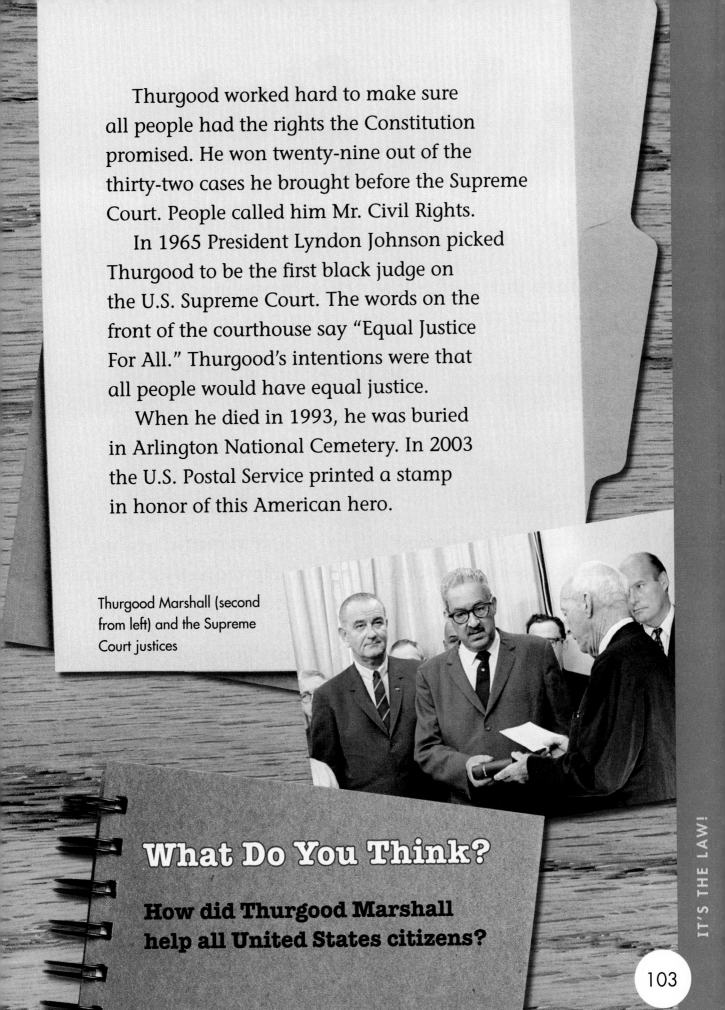

Thurgood Marshall (second from left) and the Supreme Court justices

What Do You Think?

How did Thurgood Marshall help all United States citizens?

Silly State Laws

Read some strange state laws below. Maybe at one time these laws made sense. Now they just make us laugh.

NORTH

In **Alaska,** it is against the law to disturb a sleeping bear to take its photograph.

In **Vermont,** you are not allowed to try to whistle underwater.

In **North Dakota,** you cannot fall asleep with your shoes on.

In **Michigan,** you may not tie an alligator to a fire hydrant.

In **Georgia,**
chickens must not
cross highways.

In **Alabama,**
you can't train a bear
to wrestle.

In **Florida,**
you'd better not get
caught jogging with
your eyes shut.

In **Tennessee,**
it is unlawful to catch
fish with a lasso.

In **Massachusetts,** gorillas can't ride in the back seats of cars.

In **Virginia,** chickens must not lay eggs before 8 A.M. or after 4 P.M.

In **Connecticut,** dogs can't be educated.

In **New Jersey,** it is against the law to slurp your soup.

In **California,**
you can't ride a bike
in a swimming pool.

In a city in **Colorado,**
it is illegal to let dandelions
grow within the city limits.

In a city in **Utah,** don't
forget to bring back your
library books. You can go
to jail for a month if you
don't return a library book.

In **Nevada,**
you can be fined if
you forget to close
your gate.

4 you 2 Do

Word Play

Synonyms are words that have similar meanings. Read the words below. Match the words on the left with the correct synonym on the right.

intention	demand
pollution	irritate
require	interrupt
annoy	work together
cooperate	litter
disturb	purpose

Making Connections

Why is it important to have laws, even if they don't make everyone happy?

On Paper

If you suddenly became "Boss of the World," what are some of the first laws you would make?

Answers for Word Play: intention/purpose; pollution/litter; require/demand; annoy/irritate; cooperate/work together; disturb/interrupt

POETRY

POETRY

Words 2 the Wise

Poetry is a different way to express ourselves. Think about poetry you've heard or read as you read this week's selections.

Let's Explore

Poetry

Ogden Nash is famous for his funny poems and made-up words.

Be on the lookout for poems! They are everywhere. They are on buses. They are in songs. Poetry teaches you to look at old things in new ways. Sometimes they cause people to feel an emotion.

Langston Hughes was an African American poet. He wrote poems about African American culture.

Poems say a lot in a few words. Sometimes poems compare two things such as *ideas fizzle like soda, hair as black as licorice*, or *eyes sparkle like diamonds*.

Poets choose words for their sounds. Poetry, like music, should be heard. Read a poem aloud. This will help you hear how words sound together. The words may rhyme like *think* and *drink*. Or they may begin with the same sound like *sad* and *silk*. Poems also have rhythm like *Twinkle, Twinkle, Little Star*.

Mother Goose stories have a simple rhyme to them.

Poets play with words. Sometimes they create new words. *Hock-Zocker court, Mop-Noodled Finch,* and *Thinker-Upper* are new word creations. What do you think they could mean?

Dr. Seuss plays with words when he writes poems about these characters.

BRINGING WORDS TO LIFE

by Sophia Caribacas

Poetry can be a way to say something with a few words. Poets use strong action words like *devour* instead of *eat*. *I devour pizza!* They compare things like eyes and stars. They both twinkle. *Her eyes twinkled like stars in the night sky.* They sometimes use words that rhyme. *Stars are bright. They shine at night.* They repeat sounds like the letters in the phrase *the soft sunset.* Poets create a rhythm.

Poets perform on stage at a poetry slam.

Poetry can come alive when performed onstage.

Poetry slams have become a way for poets to share their ideas. In a poetry slam, people perform a poem in front of an audience. Slams are different from poetry readings. Slams are contests. Poems are judged.

The judges are chosen from the audience. There are usually three rounds. The poets with the best scores move on to the next round. Poets only have three minutes. The judges take away points if a poet goes over three minutes.

These poets have to work on what they say. They also have to work on *how* they say it. They can use their bodies. They can use their faces. Most importantly, they use their voices. Their voices give emotion to their poetry.

Performing poetry in front of an audience isn't new. It existed before writing did. It has existed for thousands of years. Early poets memorized their poems. They used poems to share stories.

The words and rhythm of the poem carry a strong message.

Words and actions help poets connect with the audience.

POETRY SLAMS

Poetry slams are very popular today. They started in Chicago in 1984. People started sharing their poems in front of an audience. And the audience liked to hear poetry.

The first national slam was held in 1990. Now there are about 75 poetry teams. They come from many countries. Poetry slam teams often have unique names. A team from New York is called Mouth Almighty. The Columbus Thunderpants is a team from Ohio.

POETRY

Most poetry slams are at neighborhood coffee shops. They are also at bookstores. Poets perform there. These places are cozy and comfortable. Imagine candles lit on the tables. Imagine an audience who wants to listen. It can be like talking with your family! Most times, the audience doesn't clap. If people like a poem, they snap their fingers.

Reading a poem for an audience can be very exciting.

120

Poetry slams are popular in many schools.

Poetry slams are not only for adults. Kids all over the world express emotion in poetry slams. They like to tell about the first day of school. They like to tell about home. They like to tell how they made a soccer goal. Kids like to tell about life.

At poetry slams people can say what is on their
minds. They can express themselves. WritersCorps
works to get kids involved. The WritersCorps sends
poets and writers to schools. These people get students
excited about poems. They help students write and
perform poetry. Then, students can become part of
the national Youth Poetry Slam League. They get a
chance to perform their poetry in a national slam.

You can start at school too. Talk to your teacher about having a poetry slam. Ask your friends. Start with a small group. Try performing your favorite poems. Or try performing poems written by famous poets. You'll make the words come alive!

WHAT DO YOU THINK?

Why would somebody like to participate in a poetry slam?

Amy the Shy

by Peggy Russell
illustrated by
Karen Stormer Brooks

"The annual school art show is next week, and I need to know what piece of art each of you will enter. Remember, be creative!" Mrs. Key said.

Oh, no! Amy thought. *I still don't have anything to enter.*

"What piece will you enter, DeeDee?" Mrs. Key asked.

"I don't know yet," she replied.

"Hmm. Amy, what is your piece going to be?" Mrs. Key asked.

"I don't have one," Amy said.

"Well then you two can work together," Mrs. Key said. "DeeDee, you can compose music to go with Amy's poem," Mrs. Key said. "It will be a great contribution to the show."

There is no way I can read a poem in front of all those people, Amy thought. I'll freeze. Everyone will laugh.

"Mrs. Key, I can't perform with Amy. She's way too shy," DeeDee complained.

"I'm sure you will both find a way to work it out," Mrs. Key said.

DeeDee sat next to Amy at lunch. "Did you bring your poems?" DeeDee asked.

Amy handed her a notebook.

"Which poem do you want to perform?" DeeDee asked.

"I wish Mrs. Key skipped me. Everyone is going to laugh at me," Amy said.

DeeDee flipped through the notebook. "My Garden, My Room, I Like Purple," she read. "You certainly compose lots of poems."

Amy nodded.

"And you certainly don't talk much," DeeDee said.

Amy's face felt warm.

"Mrs. Key said we had to make a plan," she said.

This won't work, Amy thought.

DeeDee flipped through the pages in Amy's notebook. "Here's one! It's perfect!" she said.

Amy looked at the page in DeeDee's hand. "I don't know," she said softly.

"Would you recite the poem for me?" Amy asked.

"If I'm busy reading, who will make the sound effects?" DeeDee asked. "We should each do what we are good at. Let's practice."

DeeDee tapped a beat with her foot. "Go ahead. You can start anytime," she said.

Amy started to recite in a delicate voice. "I'm shy. I don't know why."

DeeDee stopped tapping. "I can't hear a word you're saying. You have to talk much louder than that," she said.

"It's no use," Amy said. "I'm never going to be able to read this poem in front of an audience."

"You can do this. Let's try it again," DeeDee said.

DeeDee tapped her foot to the beat. She made sound effects and clapped her hands.

Amy read the poem again. While DeeDee listened, she started to think that the art show was going to be a total disaster.

When the day of the art show finally arrived, DeeDee told Amy in a delicate way, "Don't worry. I have a plan."

"Please say this when it's our turn," DeeDee said. She handed Mrs. Key a piece of paper.

"Our final performance piece this evening is by Amy the Shy and DeeDee the Sly," Mrs. Key said.

The girls took their places on stage. DeeDee started tapping. Amy opened her mouth, but nothing came out.

The students waited. DeeDee handed Amy a large sign as she tap danced. The sign read "I am shy."

"She's shy," sang DeeDee. She handed Amy another sign. It read, "I don't know why."

"She doesn't know why," DeeDee sang. DeeDee had made signs for each line in Amy's poem.

Everyone enjoyed the show.

"I can't believe you put my poem on signs. You saved our performance," Amy said afterwards.

"What can I say? We make a good team," DeeDee said.

What Do You THINK?

Could Amy have performed without DeeDee's help?

Be a Poet

Plan for a Poetry Slam

Your class can hold a poetry slam. Here's how:

1. **Ask** When would be a good time for the whole audience? Choose a day and a time for your slam.

2. **Ask** Whom will we invite? Make invitations.

3. **Ask** What poem says something important? Have each person choose a poem to perform.

4. **Ask** How will I use my voice? Decide how you will perform the poem. Make sure it doesn't go over three minutes. Begin practicing.

5. **Ask** Who would be a good host? Choose a host to introduce each artist and keep time.

6. **Ask** What do we use to rate the poets?
Have everyone write down their picks for the top three artists. Count the votes and announce the winners.

7. **Ask** What would be a good prize? Give prizes such as ribbons, notepads or fancy pencils.

Tips for Reading Poetry

- Read the title. Does it tell you what the poem's about?

- Read the poem aloud. Listen to the sounds of the words. Which words are most important?

- Try to understand the poem using your own words instead of the poet's words.

- Is the poem too hard to understand? Choose another one!

4 YOU 2 DO

Word Play

Sometimes poets make up their poems without much planning. Say a short sentence using the words below. Be creative!

rhythm

delicate

emotion

Making Connections

How is DeeDee and Amy's talent show act like a poetry slam?

On Paper

Some poets are too shy to read their poetry. Some like to act out their poems. Others like to sing their poems. How would you perform your poetry? Write about your performance.

Glossary

a·dopt (ə dopt´), *VERB.* to take something for your own or as your own choice; accept: *Heather's family will adopt a dog today.* **a·dopt·ed, a·dopt·ing.**

a·muse (ə myüz´), *VERB.* to cause to laugh or smile: *She will amuse him with her jokes.* **a·mused, a·mus·ing.**

an·noy (ə noi´), *VERB.* to make angry; disturb: *Bugs annoy me.* **an·noyed, an·noy·ing.**

cap·ture (kap´ chər), *VERB.* take by force; to make a prisoner: *We will capture butterflies with a net.* **cap·ture, cap·tur·ing.**

com·fort (kum´ fərt), *NOUN.* someone or something that makes life easier: *You were a great comfort to me while I was sick.*

com·pose (kəm pōz′), *VERB.* to put a work of art together, using words, sounds, and colors: *Musicians use notes to compose songs.* **com·posed, com·pos·ing.**

co·op·e·rate (kō op′ ə rāt′), *VERB.* to work together: *We should all cooperate and clean up after the class party.* **co·op·e·rat·ed, co·op·e·rat·ing.**

cre·ate (krē āt′), *VERB.* to make something which has not been made before: *She wants to create music.* **cre·at·ed, cre·at·ing.**

a in hat	ō in open	sh in she
ā in age	ȯ in all	th in thin
â in care	ô in order	ᴛʜ in then
ä in far	oi in oil	zh in measure
e in let	ou in out	⎧ a in about
ē in equal	u in cup	⎪ e in taken
ėr in term	u̇ in put	ə = ⎨ i in pencil
i in it	ü in rule	⎪ o in lemon
ī in ice	ch in child	⎩ u in circus
o in hot	ng in long	

del·i·cate (del´ ə kit), *ADJECTIVE.*
1. fragile; thin; easily torn: *A spider web is very delicate.*
2. pleasing to see, touch, or taste; mild or soft: *This sweater is very delicate.*

dis·play (dis plā´), *NOUN.* a public showing; exhibit: *Have you seen the museum's display of new paintings?*

dis·turb (dis tėrb´), *VERB.* to bother a person by talking or by being noisy; interrupt: *Do not disturb the sleeping baby.* **dis·turbed, dis·turb·ing.**

e·mo·tion (i mō´ shən), *NOUN.* a strong feeling of any kind: *Love, anger, and excitement are emotions.*

e·nor·mous (i nôr´ məs), *ADJECTIVE.* very, very large; huge: *Cleaning the garage will be an enormous task.*

ex·er·cise (ek´ sər sīz), *NOUN.* the use of the body to improve it; working out: *The athlete runs a mile in the morning as his exercise.*

ex·press (ek spres´), *VERB.* to show something by your look, voice, or action: *A smile can express joy.* **ex·pressed, ex·press·ing.**

in·spire (in spīr´), *VERB.*
1. to cause someone to do something good: *His poor grade inspired him to study harder for the next test.*
2. to cause a good thought or a good feeling in someone: *The leader's courage inspired confidence in others.* **in·spired, in·spir·ing.**

a in hat	ō in open	sh in she
ā in age	ȯ in all	th in thin
â in care	ô in order	ŦH in then
ä in far	oi in oil	zh in measure
e in let	ou in out	⎧ a in about
ē in equal	u in cup	⎪ e in taken
ėr in term	u̇ in put	ə = ⎨ i in pencil
i in it	ü in rule	⎪ o in lemon
ī in ice	ch in child	⎩ u in circus
o in hot	ng in long	

in·ten·tion (in ten´ shən), NOUN. a plan, goal, or purpose that you have: *Our intention is to travel next summer.*

lib·er·ty (lib´ ər tē), NOUN. freedom: *In 1865, the United States granted liberty to all people who were slaves.* PL. **lib·er·ties.**

mon·u·ment (mon´ yə mənt), NOUN. something such as a building, pillar, statue, or stone that is set up to honor a person or an event: *The Statue of Liberty is a monument to freedom.*

po·et·ry (pō´ i trē), NOUN. poems: *We enjoy hearing our teacher read poetry.*

pol·lu·tion (pə lü´ shən), NOUN. anything that dirties an environment: *Pollution in the lake harms the fish.*

pres·i·dent (prez′ ə dənt), *NOUN.* the leader of a country, business, or other group: *The first president of the United States was George Washington.*

pro·vide (prə vīd′), *VERB.* to give something that is needed or wanted: *The school will provide supplies to the students.* **pro·vid·ed, pro·vid·ing.**

re·cite (ri sīt′), *VERB.*

1. to say something from memory, especially in front of an audience: *He will recite several poems.*
2. to tell about something in detail: *She will recite her adventures at camp.* **re·cit·ed, re·cit·ing.**

re·quire (ri kwīr′), *VERB.*

1. to need: *Some plants require sunshine to grow.*
2. to say that you have to do something: *The rules require us all to be at school on time.* **re·quired, re·quir·ing.**

a in hat	ō in open	sh in she
ā in age	ȯ in all	th in thin
â in care	ô in order	ᵀH in then
ä in far	oi in oil	zh in measure
e in let	ou in out	⌠a in about
ē in equal	u in cup	⎪e in taken
ėr in term	u̇ in put	ə={ i in pencil
i in it	ü in rule	⎪o in lemon
ī in ice	ch in child	⌡u in circus
o in hot	ng in long	

rhythm (riᴛʜˊ əm), *NOUN.* a strong beat that some music or poetry has: *We tapped our feet and clapped our hands to the rhythm of the music.*

sculp·tor (skulpˊ tər), *NOUN.* an artist who makes things by cutting or shaping them: *The sculptor made a statue that is now in a museum.*

strug·gle (strugˊ əl), *VERB.* to try hard; work hard against difficulties: *The dog will struggle to get away from a stranger.* **strug·gled, strug·gling.**

sym·bol (simˊ bəl), *NOUN.* something that stands for something else: *The bald eagle is a symbol of the United States.*

the·a·ter (thēˊ ə tər), *NOUN.* a place where people go to see movies or plays: *We saw the movie at the new theater.*

Acknowledgments

Illustrations

3, 59, 70–76, 138 Susan Tolonen; **28–29** Gary Phillips; **44–50** Daniel Powers; **104–107** Shane McGowan; **124–130** Karen Stormer Brooks

Photographs

Every effort has been made to secure permission and provide appropriate credit for photographic material. The publisher deeply regrets any omission and pledges to correct errors called to its attention in subsequent editions.

Unless otherwise acknowledged, all photographs are the property of Scott Foresman, a division of Pearson Education.

Photo locators denoted as follows: Top (T), Center (C), Bottom (B), Left (L), Right (R), Background (Bkgd).

Opener: (BR) ©Royalty-Free/Corbis, (TR) ©Scott Montgomery/Getty Images, (L) Getty Images; **1** Getty Images; **2** (TL) Visual Language Illustration, (TR) ©Reza Estakhrian/Getty Images, (BR) ©Bob Elsdale/Getty Images; **3** Getty Images; **5** ©Royalty-Free/Corbis; **6** (TR) ©Reza Estakhrian/Getty Images, (R) Visual Language Illustration, (BR) ©Hugh Sitton/Getty Images; **7** Getty Images; **8** Getty Images; **9** (L) ©Riccardo Savi/Getty Images, (T) ©Ken Biggs/Getty Images; **10** (Bkgd) ©Ken Biggs/Getty Images, (BC) ©Reza Estakhrian/Getty Images; **11** Getty Images; **12** ©AbleStock/IndexOpen; **13** (TL) ©Bettmann/Corbis, (BR) ©Rachel Watson/Getty Images, (TL) Getty Images; **14** (BL, R) ©Hulton Archive/Getty Images, (C) Getty Images; **15** ©Dennis Hallinan/Getty Images; **16** ©Museum of the City of New York/Corbis; **17** (TL) ©Hugh Sitton/Getty Images, (BR) ©Hulton Archive/Getty Images; **18** ©Hulton Archive/Getty Images; **19** Getty Images; **20** (B) Getty Images, (TR) ©Underwood & Underwood/Corbis, (TR) Visual Language Illustration; **21** Visual Language Illustration; **22** (TR) Visual Language Illustration, (CL) ©Kathie Larsen/Getty Images; **23** (TR) ©Bernstein Collection/Corbis, (BR) ©Buddy Mays/Corbis; **24** (CL) ©Bettmann/Corbis, (TR) Visual Language Illustration; **25** (BC) ©Dave Bartruff/Corbis, (TR) ©Popperfoto/Alamy Images, (TR) Visual Language Illustration; **26** ©Hulton Archive/Getty Images; **27** (L, B) Visual Language Illustration; **28** ©Chris Collins/Corbis; **29** ©Ariel Skelley/Corbis; **30** Getty Images; **31** ©Bob Elsdale/Getty Images; **32** (TR) ©Tim Flach/Getty Images, (CR) Stockdisc, (BR) ©Eastcott Momatiuk/Getty Images; **33** ©Blend Images/Getty Images; **34** ©Tim Flach/Getty Images; **35** (BL) ©Mike Hill/Getty Images, (CR) ©Betsie van der Meer/Getty Images, (Bkgd) Getty Images; **36** Stockdisc; **37** (CR) Getty Images, (C) ©Ursula Klawitter/Corbis; **38** (B) ©Corbis, (C) ©Royalty-Free/Corbis; **38** Getty Images; **39** Stockdisc; **40** (BC) ©Ariel Skelley/Corbis, (TC) Corbis; **41** (TL, TR, BR, BL) Getty Images, (BC) ©Karen Beard/Getty Images, (BC) ©Pat Doyle/Corbis; **42** ©Paul Sounders/Corbis; **43** (R) Getty Images, (CR) ©Blend Images/Getty Images; **53** ©Royalty-Free/Corbis; **55** ©Eastcott Momatiuk/Getty Images; **56** (TL, BL) Getty Images; **57** ©Rosanne Olsen/Getty Images; **58** (TR) ©Steve Ewert Photography, (BR) Getty Images; **60** ©John Francis/Getty Images; **61** (T) ©Dan Bigelow/Getty Images, (B) ©Tim Flach/Getty Images; **62** ©Michael Brosilow Photography; **63** ©Steve Ewert Photography; **64** ©Michael Brosilow Photography; **65** ©Michael Brosilow Photography; **66** (CL, TR) ©Steve Ewert Photography; **67** ©Michael Brosilow Photography; **68** (BC) ©Steve Ewert Photography, (TL) ©Gabe Palmer/Alamy; **69** ©Michael Brosilow Photography; **79** ©Steve Hamblin/Alamy; **83** ©Barros & Barros/Getty Images; **84** (TR, BR, BC) Getty Images, (CR) Corbis; **85** ©Rob Howard/Corbis; **86** Getty Images; **87** Getty Images; **88** ©GDT/Getty Images; **89** Getty Images; **90** (BL) Getty Images, (BC) Jupiter Images, (BR) Stockdisc; **91** Stockdisc, (BL) ©CSA Plastock/Getty Images, (BR) Getty Images, (BC) ©Alan Schein/Corbis; **92** (TC) Stockdisc, (T) ©Viennaphoto/Alamy Images; **94** (TR) ©Martin Jones/Corbis, (CR) ©Tim Davis/Getty Images, (Bkgd) ©Bernd Mellmann/Alamy Images; **95** (TL) ©Royalty-Free/Corbis, (CL) ©Ron Chapple/Getty Images; **96** (TR) Corbis, (Bkgd, C, TL) Getty Images; **97** (BR, T, BC, Bkgd) Getty Images; **98** (C, TL) Getty Images, (BL, BR) ©Bettmann/Corbis; **99** (BR, BC, TL) Getty Images, (TR) ©Bettmann/Corbis; **100** (C, BR, Bkgd) Getty Images, (B) Corbis; **101** (BC, CL, Bkgd) Getty Images, (TR) Time & Life Pictures/Getty Images; **102** (BC, TR) Getty Images, (TL) ©Bettmann/Corbis; **103** (TC, BC, Bkgd) Getty Images, (BR) ©Bettmann/Corbis; **108** (T, C) ©Bettmann/Corbis; **109** ©Royalty-Free/Corbis; **110** ©John Bryson/Getty Images; **112** ©Time & Life Pictures/Getty Images; **113** Corbis; **114** ©Marie Schubert/Corbis; **115** ©John Bryson/Getty Images; **116** ©Lisa Romerein/Getty Images; **117** ©image100/Getty Images; **118** ©Neal Preston/Corbis; **119** ©Ethno Images, Inc./Alamy Images; **120** ©Kevin Fleming/Corbis; **121** ©Anthony Marsiand/Getty Images; **122** ©Scott Montgomery/Getty Images; **123** ©Holos/Getty Images; **136** Getty Images; **140** Getty Images; **141** ©Kathie Larsen/Getty Images; **142** ©Riccardo Savi/Getty Images